CELEBRATE CHRISTMAS ANEW

Robert Scrivner

LUCIDBOOKS

Contents

Incarnation

In Father's heart of love was born,
The grandeur of LOVE's Story.
In Mary's womb was Truth conceived,
And we beheld His glory!

He's the glory of the Father,
In human flesh arrayed.
God's eternal Lamb Bethlehem born—
Yeshua ha Mashiach to earth conveyed.

Yeshua, Abba's Eden Seed—
Creator by Holy Spirit power—
As Isaiah prophesied, He came,
This Incarnate Deliverer ours!

Abundant Christmas

Take possession of God's abundance.
Let all God's children believe,
There is bounty sent from heaven,
Flowing to all who will receive.

Let the devil's kingdom be shaken—
His fake dominion be fully disclosed.
Such a sham Satan lives. What a shame Satan is,
Still controlling your money, since Jesus disrobed.

"Jesus made a show of him openly,"
Is the way the Scriptures express,
The fall of this one to Jehovah the Son,
Before hell's host in outer darkness.

Celebrate with me the Savior's birth.
Rejoice Messiah reigns heaven's Lord.
God's first Christmas night was a total delight.
Abundance is God's good Christmas word.

Almighty Redeemer Savior Supreme

Jesus our Savior Master of all,
You have come here to bow in Bethlehem's stall.
Almighty Redeemer, Savior Supreme,
We worship You ever. Your praises we sing.

Born in a manger—no room in the inn—
You have come here to save. We welcome You in.
Come alive in our hearts. Let Your kingdom begin.
Our Lord Messiah, reign Savior within.

Mary and Joseph beside You take rest.
True servants, they here the God-Son caress.
Savior Redeemer, exalted our Lord,
Reign mightily within, by new hearts adored.

Assignment Bethlehem

Above the hills of Bethlehem,
The angels voiced God's joy:
"Tonight the Captain of the host,
Is born a baby Boy!

This is that day men prophesied,
In timeless Ransom Story,
For here this night to My delight,
Is birthed My Son of glory.

In David's city men shall find,
In manger bed of hay,
The Seed to bruise the serpent's head…
His might to strip away.

To loose the bound and heal the bruised,
This visitation comes.
These shepherds send to tell to men,
The birthplace of My Son!"

At Christmas in Bethlehem

It happened at Christmas in Bethlehem,
Our Messiah to Ephrata has, come.
He Father to obey is here this day.
Our Savior/Redeemer, Jehovah the Son.

Tell all earth it is true, Jesus came here for you.
To bear sins and healing Jesus here arrived.
Deliverance, preservation, and restoration He brings.
Jesus our Messiah, completely transformed our lives.
Jesus humanity unconditionally redeemed.

Celebrate with me at Christmas the birth,
Of Jesus—heavenly host commander—extreme.
Here for our sins and soon coming again,
Let us celebrate Christmas eternally redeemed.

As a Baby Jesus came, then lived as a man.,
Proclaiming freedom and restoration in Galilee.
Then to Jerusalem bound, He laid His life down,
That Christmas celebrants might be totally free!

At Christmas Jesus Is Born

Mary, Joseph, and Jesus—God the Son—
Thanks for Your obedience. This night is the one,
When earth will know the glory of God,
As Jesus, for our freedom, to this earth comes.

Not everyone kneels at the cradle of Jesus,
But all will bow at the throne of God.
For at Christmas Jesus as Savior came.
Destined for the Cross, to shed salvation Blood.

At Christmas Jesus came for Easter,
All Jesus did, was prelude to Resurrection Morn.
Celebrate Christmas with Joseph and Mary—
Reverently worship God. At Christmas Jesus is born.

Barn-Born Savior of Men

Travel with me to Bethlehem.
Look over there! It is Mary.
Joseph with her the donkey leads.
What is that bundle Mary carries?

Look swaddling clothes and a baby blanket.
She has come prepared for the imminent time.
She looks tired and Joseph seems anxious.
Where will they ever room find.

They need room for this soon-born Jesus.
Warm beds and a bath for dust.
They have God obeyed. To pay taxes they come.
Where will they find a place to bear Jesus.

Is God listening to His servant Mary?
Does He have a safe house for His Son?
See Joseph knocking; searching, he asks,
Is there room for my wife? Her baby soon comes.

Yes! Out in the back with animals will do.
The stable is where His birth will be.
In this place, the world will view God's grace.
Jesus, our barn-born Savior, will set all sinners free.

The Bethlehem Gospel to Tell

Jesus has fully disrobed Satan.
Jesus has all hell's hordes defeated.
Our redemption is done. Our victory is won.
Salvation in human flesh is completed.

Declared in Jerusalem as Jesus Son of God,
Christmas is rejoicing with Joseph and Mary.
With Simeon and Anna we recognize,
Mary has to us Jehovah-Son carried.

Christmas is celebration of our Lord Christ.
Christmas is rejoicing with Mary and angels.
Christmas is shouting, "Jesus has arrived!"
Jesus came, God's Bethlehem Gospel to tell.

Bethlehem Savior

"To you a Savior is born," the angels conveyed.
Jehovah here bows as Son. He is in Bethlehem laid.
Yes, God's holy Son as Redeemer here comes.
Go worship Him fully…Yeshua God's Son.

To Bethlehem come is Israel's King.
As Savior he humbly lays in Bethlehem straw.
What a Deliverer/Redeemer supreme!
We lift worship, offer praise, give Him laud.

Jehovah, Yeshua, Redeemer, great Lamb,
As we bow at your manger, your resurrection is our stand.
Descended from your throne our sin to atone,
To save, heal and prosper us, you have come.

Bethlehem-Savior, Redeemer-Messiah-Son,
No other One comes to make us live pure.
Your Christmas arrival is love beyond all.
Bethlehem born Savior, our futures You secure.

Born in Bethlehem

A Savior is born in Bethlehem.
A Savior is born this night.
He is the King of all creation.
In our Jehovah Jesus is might.

We will worship Him King in Bethlehem,
Nazareth, Galilee, and all Judea.
We will praise His Name and fully proclaim,
This Savior comes to free us.

Savior, Almighty Deliverer,
In Bethlehem born to us this day.
We honor you. We give You awe.
Your will to save us, we obey.

Jesus our Redeemer, Savior,
Almighty Messiah Lord,
We praise Your Name. Your love we claim.
You, our Deliverer, we forever adore.

Born in Bethlehem— Jerusalem's Crown

Born in Bethlehem—Jerusalem's Crown.
Born in Bethlehem, from heaven come down.
Born in Bethlehem, Jesus Messiah for me.
Born in Bethlehem, heaven sent jubilee.

King of Creation and Lord of all lords,
Highest in earth and heaven adored.
Yeshua ha Mashiach, Redeemer great Friend,
Lord of the Ages, Salvation He sends.

Who will assemble at Bethlehem's manger?
Who will find Christ their Redeemer arranger?
Let all of creation bow at the Name,
Of the Lord God Eternal, our Savior Who came.

Jesus our Lord, our opulent Creator,
Alpha and Omega, Redeemer and Savior.
We praise You. We worship. We exalt You our Lord,
Come to Redeem us, we offer You love. Be ever adored.

Born to You a Savior

On a hillside near Bethlehem of Ephrata,
Shepherds silently grazed their sheep.
Suddenly there shown a golden glow.
As shepherds watched, they heard angels speak:

"Glory to God in the highest our praise,
Born to you this night is a Savior.
Rise and worship. Make haste to Bethlehem.
With Mary and Joseph honor this Child from forever!"

Mary pondered in her heart these shepherds' praise.
As she hugged her Son—God's holy One,
She was thinking, Jerusalem is the proper place,
To present Jesus the Savior, God's Son.

Simeon be blessed. We accept your praise.
This Child shall in Israel be Lord and King—
A Light to shine to the nations always.
Dear Anna, Jesus celebrate. Sweet praises bring.

Bring Him High Honor

Born in Bethlehem, Savior and Lord.
Let Jesus be worshipped and highly adored.
This One Who is Savior—Boy-Child born King—
To His reborn, restoration and healing brings.

Who will bow low to God's Boy-King here?
Who will bring honor and His presence revere?
Jesus the Christ Child, Jehovah's sent Son,
Lord of Creation—from Heaven—is come.

Bring Him high honor. Sing to Him high praise.
Worship Him. Honor Him. His love anthem raise.
There is none like Yeshua, Creator and Lord,
The highest of heaven, lowly, here much adored.

Mary and Joseph you are pleasing to God.
Soon Jesus of Nazareth will offer His Blood,
For the sins of the nations and Salvation of all.
Master, Healer, Redeemer, before You we fall!

By Jesus Christ of Christmas

Let Christmas be a reminding remembrance,
Of the love and might of your God.
In December remember the mighty power
Of Jesus' redeeming, healing Blood.

Let each Christmas be your empowering anew.
With Pentecost power be newly enflamed.
Be reminded of the place you encountered God's grace,
Praise glorious might of His saving/healing Name.

In December's holy month of Christmas,
Be re-united with your Savior anew.
Remember Jesus came to give you His Name.
He with Pentecost strength will daily endue.

Christmas, Easter, and Pentecost might,
Was first revealed in God's Earth-born Son.
Pentecost power and authority is yours today,
By Jesus Christ of Christmas, God's will in you be done!

Celebrate the Birth

When you open your Christmas presents,
Know Jesus came to Bethlehem for you.
Celebrate the birth of the Savior of Earth.
Rejoice in His great love most true.

Tell your children their Savior's Name.
He is Jesus the Christ of Christmas.
Worship Father God, for Jesus has come.
Know your grandchildren will never be lost.

Each Christmas morning choose to rejoice,
That Jesus has come to Earth for you.
Make it a yearly cherished celebration.
In His manger see liberation true.

Think yearly on the town of Bethlehem,
Where in obedience Joseph came,
With Mary His bride. Celebrate Jesus' birth,
That all the world might be changed.

Celebrate Christmas

Celebrate Christmas with Jesus the Babe.
Celebrate Easter with Jesus the Man.
Celebrate Pentecost with the Jesus-sent Spirit.
Christmas is eternal celebration,
When with Jesus the Redeemer you stand.

Merry Christmas to all in every land!
In Jesus know eternal delight!
Celebrate Christmas the Jesus way.
Christmas is Easter—the very first night.

Christmas is the best of all seasons.
There is grace with power in Jesus the Lamb.
The blessed Son of God shed holy Blood.
Celebrate Christmas! Be Christ's to command!

Celebrate Christmas Anew

Yield to God a Christmas gift!
Give to God the gift of you.
Lift your praise and worship to Christ,
As you celebrate Christmas anew!

Give God every crevice of your life.
In your spirit, let love reign evermore.
Give to Father God great Christmas joy.
Let God your total being restore.

God gave Himself at Christmas!
From God's heart came Heaven's Best.
God Incarnate came to a Bethlehem stall,
The Ever-Giving Heart of God to express.

Christmas is celebration of Christ, in giving.
Won't you give yourself completely to Jesus?
Give to your family and to God great joy—
Celebrate every Christmas with Father, in Jesus!

Celebrate Christmas! Christ Is Born!

Celebrate today God's Christmas joy.
Welcome Yeshua Mashiach Prince in.
Not many years hence, this Jewish Prince,
Shall present Yahweh's peace to men.

Bring to Jerusalem's walls God's holy love,
Rejoice in peace all people in lands beyond.
Your Lord has come as Jehovah the Son.
He will lift Redemption's eternal song!

Celebrate Christmas! Christ Jesus is born!
While lowly shepherds heed angel chorus,
"In Bethlehem's stable lays the Savior of men.
He is humbly bringing God's love before us!"

From Nazareth to Bethlehem's crib,
Our Savior to be born was carried.
Let Jesus our Lord be highly adored.
Bowing low, give kudos to Joseph and Mary!

Celebrate the King of Heaven

When I knelt before God's holy throne,
I saw Jesus my Redeemer there.
In total victory risen, Jesus was ever livin',
His Father's great throne to share.

Jesus the Almighty from Earth had returned,
Now in Heaven, He sat...the Eternal One.
Yes! The great rescuing King on Heaven's throne,
Is Jehovah our Messiah—God the Son.

Down from His throne to Bethlehem,
Jesus bowed low that first Christmas night.
It was a holy scene. Jehovah just beamed.
As He saw many in His Savior-Son delight.

Angels on a Judean hillside had decreed,
"On Earth peace, goodwill toward men!"
Mary, and Joseph, knelt beside Baby Jesus' manger.
All God told of the Child, was true in Bethlehem.

Yes, that Baby seen resting in Bethlehem's hay,
Is now our Redeemer on heaven's grand throne.
No longer a Child, Jesus has reconciled,
All who Bow—making Heaven's King their own.

Celebrate the Lord

True-Christmas sing to every land—
The Christmas Christ proclaim.
Share the great I AM from Bethlehem.
Yeshua LORD…His Name.

Join in Celebration of the Christ—
The Mass of Christ's Grand Worth.
Bow before this Prince of Peace,
Born King to save the earth!

Celebrate the Lord—this newborn Christ.
Bow to worship; to praise; to adore.
Crown Christmas Christ, your King of Peace,
Your Redeemer…your Savior…your LORD!

Christmas-Abundance-Blessing

To LIFE! To LIFE!...our *Christ*mas praise.
We are, "Glory to God in the Highest!" saved.
Thank You! Thank You! Zoe King,
For this *Life of God* You gave!

*Christ*mas is our Feast of God's New Wine.
The Anointing One is our spirits empowering.
For Abundant Life, the Anointed has come—
Lack, sickness, and sin devouring!

We celebrate in Christ, the Spirit of Might—
*Christ*mas anointing, unhindered out flowing.
The Seed of Abraham, the Sin-Curse breaks—
*Christ*mas-Abundance-Blessing bestowing!

Christmas-Born Freedom

In Lord Yeshua-God Man-Messiah,
For mankind full freedom abounds.
Freedom from hell…made right…whole and well,
As the wealth of heaven flows down.

Since the Sovereign from heaven descended,
To the earth, through Mary that night,
We as Abraham's seed, abundantly freed,
In our Christmas-born freedom delight.

Now we echo angelic host rhapsody,
Our full freedom in Christ melody.
We exalt this Babe, God's Anointed of Love
Whom the sin of all repenting ones removes.

Now by the Sovereign of Heaven, love crowned,
Our full freedom in life is unbound.
For none can restrain the shalom redeemed,
As they live in Shalom Prince, as earth-kings!

The Christmas Christ Know

If to gain eternity you would give,
The Christmas Christ just one minute,
You could receive His gift of eternal joy,
That includes life in heaven in your private mansion.

Do not let your eternal joy be lost,
By rejecting Christmas Christ and His Life-giving Cross.
Bow at Christmas. Receive your gleaming-white
righteous robe.
In Jesus gain life, joy and peace of eternal redemption.

As bright as diamonds, a diadem of deity receive.
The great gift of glorious light beaming two millennium ago,
From the Crown of Creations redeeming brow just for you.
Be changed by His love forever.
You can now the Christmas Christ know.

Christmas Christ's Anointing-One Filled

You cannot fully honor the Christmas Babe,
Without Christ's Anointing-One in you.
You are twice born by faith in the Blood of Christ,
Now be Christ's Anointing-One endued.

Be you being filled this day with the
Holy-Anointing-One-Spirit.
To heaven and earth's Shekinah yield.
Be Power-of-Pentecost Christmas-flamed.
Be the Christmas Christ's Anointing-One filled.

Be anointed by God the Holy Spirit.
Be the true Spirit of Christmas obeying.
A life of love and power then yours,
You will be fully equipped to serve.
The birth might of Jesus conveying.

Christmas Christ— Mankind's Liberty

A joyous Christmas poem I'll write,
That tells Jehovah's great love.
How He sent His Son—His precious One—
As Savior our sins to remove.

I'll write how Mary took Gabriel's word,
That she should bear God's Savior Son.
For this virgin engaged to Joseph bore,
Son of the Highest by the Spirit here come.

In Bethlehem born as prophesied,
The Messiah was to shepherds revealed.
As the angels rejoiced shepherds received,
Son of God to save and sickness heal.

Let us rejoice today with heaven's host.
God the Son shall highly exalted be.
Jesus will evermore be greatly adored…
As Christ of Christmas—mankind's liberty!

Christmas Freedom Eternally Lasts

Worship with me the Savior of men,
Barn-born behind the Bethlehem inn.
Jesus the Messiah to the earth has come—
Here to rescue from enslavement to sin.

Humble shepherds on Judean hillside,
As confirming witnesses were called:
"To Bethlehem go that the world may know,
Salvation lies in Bethlehem's stall."

God's world can be free from sinning now.
Their guilt may now lie in their past.
For to all this day a Savior is born.
Christmas freedom eternally lasts.

Christmas in All the Earth

Rejoice, be glad, earth-children.
Announce the Messiah's birth.
A time of cheer when God drew near,
To ransom all the earth.

First announcement came to shepherds,
"Good tidings of excellent joy,
Good news for all in every land,
This lad is Christ—God's Boy!"

With shepherds and later wise men,
We proclaim Messiah's birth.
Our songs of praise to heaven we raise.
It is Christmas all over the earth!

Christmas Is Communion

Will you embrace your Savior?
His Spirit will you receive?
Will you be blessed by Happiness,
In Mary's womb conceived?

Will you be reconciled to God?
Will you imbibe True Grace?
Will you ingest the Living Bread,
And be His dwelling place?

Christmas is communion birthed,
Between the LORD and man.
For our complete oneness with Christ,
God formed His Christmas Plan.

Will this Celebration of the Christ,
Be the birth of your new life?
Will you be full this Christmas Day,
With the Anointing Might of Christ?

Christmas Is Jesus' Birthday

Christmas is Jesus' birthday celebration,
We celebrate His advent with joy.
Though we may have missed His coming hour,
Our elation celebration is for Heaven's Boy.

In all the Earth, in every land,
Christmas is Christ's birthday remembrance.
It could have happened in March or August,
But the date aint the issue. Give God a chance…

To be heard as omnipotent Father,
Sharing with us the birth of His Son.
Good gifts of love shared everywhere,
With Salvation—is why Jesus has come.

At Christmas observe the Christ Mass.
Let Jesus' birthday be everywhere known.
Receive all that Jesus desired for you,
Crown Jesus, Savior. Bow, count His manger His throne!

The Christmas King

We are glad for baby Jesus,
And the love He came to be.
From the throne of Father Mercy sent…
Earth's Sovereign Majesty.

As the Christmas King from heaven,
Came this gentle promised Child.
And the earth shall be His footstool,
By His Crimson reconciled.

In the coming of the Christ Child,
New hope has come to men.
For the Christmas King by ransom,
Through repentance cancels sin.

Eternal Life from heaven came,
To change man's destiny.
For the Christmas King came kneeling,
To a hill called Calvary.

The Christmas Lamb

In Bethlehem Ephrata,
The Shepherd as a Man,
By Spirit's breath in human flesh,
Became the Christmas Lamb.

Incarnate Word, from Mary's womb,
Came forth in humbled birth.
And Lamb of God, the Son of Man,
Was dwelling now on earth.

The Son of Man—the Judge of all—
In manger bed of hay,
Was born a Man to be the Lamb…
Sin's wretched wage to pay.

Because God loved the world, He came,
To Bethlehem to be…
The Lamb unblemished—bearing sins—
To set sin-captives free.

Christmas Means Celebrate Christ

Christmas time with family,
And Christmas carols with friends.
In fun, food and fellowship,
Celebration time we spend.

A time of giving presents…
Giving and receiving love.
This love we learned as children,
Messiah celebration approves.

What is this celebration?
It is a Christmas Child arrives—
Welcome to earth royal birth—
Celebration of the Christ.

Christes Maese…"Mass of Christ."
Celebrate birth of Prince Peace.
It is a Let all God's children believe,
Jesus' love celebration.
His giving-love will not cease.

The Christmas Plan

This Christmas night with stars so bright,
God's love for us shines clearly.
For from His throne God sent His Own,
To prove He loves sincerely.

For Christmas shines to Calvary,
Where Plan begun was done.
Where Christmas Babe our ransom paid,
To make of us Love sons.

Yes! Jesus Christ so innocent,
As a little Babe revealed.
Brought to earth eternal life—
God's Christmas Plan fulfilled.

Christ Mass Always

The Christ was birthed, to give *Christ* Mass always—
Our lives should be, a Christ's-Anointing celebration.
Christ's Anointing One fills our hearts Abba-love full—
Christ-love-anointed, we can become
overflowing-Zoe-fountains.

As Mount Moriah's Promised Seed, Messiah came
to Christmas.
Our hearts—His-holy-love filled—remains
Messiah's mission.
We are anointed to serve the Anointed One…
Spirit-filled to do, His Good-News-Earth Commission!

Christ Mass Celebrants

We are Christmas—*Christ* Mass—celebrants.
We bow our lives to God.
We leave our sins to enter in,
Through Christ's redeeming Blood.

Christ of Christmas—The Anointed One—
Has the Upper Room anointing released.
We honor Christ's Anointing Might—
The Holy Ghost…God of Peace.

The Prince of Peace; the anointing breathed,
"Receive ye the Holy Spirit!"
Two thousand Christmases have passed,
And still this day we hear it.

We choose this Christ—The Anointed One.
His anointing, we likewise choose.
Holy Spirit—Anointing One—
With Your might, our lives infuse.

Christmas Shalom-Freedom

Almost everyone knows about Christmas.
But just what on earth does it mean?
I am so glad you asked. It is my simple task,
To tell you of Christmas Christ, who redeems.

You don't have to be dead in your spirit. You need not cry,
Beneath the frustration perplexing your mind.
Peace means shalom—nothing missing or broken.
Christmas peace is God's promise to you. In Jesus find…

Forgiveness, of every disobedience to God.
Redeemed, means you are from sin-curse purchased back—
No longer bound by Satan, sin, fear, nor sickness.
Delivered, means freedom from bondage of any lack.

Your Christmas each year can be special,
If salvation of Christmas Christ you choose.
When the anointed Christmas Messiah liberates,
Christmas means full freedom to never lose.

Christmas...Shekinah Might Conformed

By His birth, life, death and resurrection,
Anointed Christ-Child—Hades' head defeating—
Wants us Holy One of Pentecost filled…
His Christmas-Peace Plan completing.

The Christ Mass Babe…Full-Redeemer-of-Man—
His Anointing-Wholeness Plan now completed—
Covenants to us who bear His Name,
The Shekinah-Might, Who all hell's hordes defeated.

Christmas—our Celebration of the Anointed One—
Is by LOVE's Pentecost Power transformed.
Great joy takes place as Christ's birth we embrace,
The infilling of His Anointing One confirmed.

Shekinah-Glory overshadowed the womb,
Where Easter-Triumph-Seed was sown.
Only by Christ's Shekinah-Spirit filled,
Can true glory of Christmas be known.

The Christmas Story

You have heard the story of Christmas,
With angels, shepherds and Bethlehem's stall.
Cattle, donkeys, horses, sheep, with maybe a dog or two.
There in their midst, a Babe, God's only Savior for you.

Just one entrance to heaven. Jesus' Name the only door.
We earnestly, forthrightly, daily implore.
Come bow to the Christmas Babe—God's Man
in Bethlehem.
Born of Mary by the Holy Ghost, God's only Savior for men.

One more time in the Christmas story delight,
To the lowly inn of Bethlehem, He came to save us this night.
Listen to our God in the words of this man,
Raised from the dead for you in Jerusalem.

Our Messiah preached powerfully with accompanying signs.
Many healing deliverances in Jesus we find.
Christmas shines to Easter. New hope we sing,
Let Jesus be worshipped...our exalted King.

In the Name of Jesus let the world be saved.
This Babe of Bethlehem sins fully forgave.
He healed the sick. He made the blind to see.
The Christmas story is Salvation-full, eternally!

Christ's Christmas Crimson

Christ's Christmas-crimson has set me free.
Christ's Christmas-crimson my only plea.
I will sing this song from heaven's shore,
It is Christ's Christmas-crimson for me.

Blessings from our Savior at Christmas come.
He blesses us daily in our lives.
As we praise the Name of Christmas' King,
We in His presence and power abide.

The Christmas crimson of Jesus,
Is flowing from Bethlehem to me.
I will worship Christ for all this life.
I will praise Him eternally.

The Christmas Crimson—Jesus' Blood—
Sets free from sickness and sin.
In Jesus' Christmas Crimson I am blessed,
For God the Spirit lives within.

Christ's *Christ* Mass Power

In great love, LOVE bowed,
LOVE to release—

LOVE Son
obeyed LOVE Abba.

Through LOVE the Spirit,
Abba's might is now out-flowing.

Now all the world
wholeness/peace can drink—

The Christ's
Christ Mass Power knowing!

Come Now Worship
Bow Down

Come now to Bethlehem, worship the Lamb.
Bow in the stable behind the inn.
Say to the Savior welcome, Lord, to Jerusalem.
We honor You, Lord, in Your world, life begin.

Bethlehem be commended in uplifting rhyme,
For in you God begins His search for mankind.
Throughout endless ages you ever will be,
The place where God sought humanity.

We come here to know You Jesus our Lord.
We choose in Bethlehem to honor and adore.
Our Lord be exalted! Ever be praised.
Welcome to Bethlehem, may Your world be saved!

Creator Redeemer—Now Lord—Here Below

All have heard of the twelve days of Christmas.
Some celebrate Christmas throughout December.
Having an Easter-Jesus Christmas, changes everything.
Christmas is best when the Jesus of Easter you remember.

Think, Christmas is Easter—the very first night.
Celebrate Christmas with Easter's Jesus each hour.
Think, of that very first Christmas, as our Easter-Lord
coming in might,
Giving Christmas, Easter, and Pentecost power.

Rejoice with the angels and shepherds.
Rejoice with the sheep in the stall.
Rejoice it is Christmas in Bethlehem!
Here Jesus is born Lord-Messiah, for all.

Christmas is rejoicing with vigor,
When the Jesus of Easter you know.
No other so grand as this Babe at hand—
Creator, Redeemer—now Lord—here below

A Crown to Share

To this manger a Savior comes…
To cross your sins to bear.
To this earth Jesus entered,
With you a crown to share.

Worship this Savior lying still.
Embrace your heart to His.
Declare the Christ Child reigns supreme.
Jesus in my heart shall live.

Jesus, Savior, Christ-Child, King,
Redeemer for all mankind.
The Father's glory beams in Your smile.
Radiant is your peace that floods our minds.

Jesus from Bethlehem, soon to Egypt bound,
What a wonderful Savior You are.
Soon men from the East will worship You,
As Father's great, eternal, saving Star!

Jesus eternal Savior of Bethlehem,
To the manger you came, Your love to share.
Your freedom we face, Your heart we embrace.
Father's great love for His earth we declare!

Earth-Birth of Our God

Christmas celebrates earth-birth of our God—
Who for our Salvation, visits His earth.
Here to shed for all flesh, His Redemption-pure blood.
Confirming forever, man's blood-purchased worth.

Christ Jesus, Mary's Baby-beautiful born,
You in Bethlehem slept softly that night.
How joyous our song, for to You belongs:
All creation…all glory…all might!

Earth Born in Bethlehem

We give you glory Lord and King—
Earth born in Bethlehem.
We adore you Savior for Your cross,
And Your Sunday morning resurrection.

We praise Your Name. We worship You.
We honor You, Lord, from on High.
We thank our Father that You came,
For our sins to bleed and die.

We praise You Lamb most holy,
In acclamation-love verse.
We thank You for Your holy Blood,
That ransomed from sin's curse.

We praise You Eternal Lamb of God,
For Your freedom blood flowing free.
As we honor You now, we will,
Worship You Lord, for all eternity.

Earth's Savior Here Come

We have come here to worship Jesus our Lord.
Highest honor we bring to Mary's Boy-King.
Be exalted Lord Jehovah in Bethlehem's barn.
To You Lord Messiah, Salvation-praise we sing.

We expected to find You asleep in the inn,
But You were out back with the sheep and kin.
We thought how strange for the Savior of men.
Then Joseph said, "Rest!" as he welcomed us in.

"Welcome to Bethlehem, come hold the Child,
Born Yeshua ha Mashiach, innocent and mild.
Shepherds soon come," we heard Joseph convey.
As we viewed this Child we heard Mary say…

"Gabriel said all things would be fine,
Our God gave a Son and the pleasure is mine,
To bear Him to Bethlehem, Jerusalem, and home.
We will name Him Jesus, Earth's Savior here come.

Easter's Redemption to Every Nation

Christmas is the first day of Easter—
Holy Redeemer to mankind come!
Jesus to serve is Bethlehem birthed.
In swaddling clothes, God our Savior began.

Shepherds on hillside were summoned to view,
A Savior who is Christ our Lord.
The heavens shown bright that holy night.
In Bethlehem shepherds were heard:

"We were minding our sheep—keeping faithful watch,
When a host of angels began to declare:
'Glory to God and on earth, peace, goodwill to men,
A Savior is born King in Bethlehem!'"

Christmas is the first day of Easter—
A time to rejoice in God's Salvation.
Great joy! Be it known God gives us His Own!
Christmas is Easter's Redemption to every nation!

Eternal Song of Christmas

If I had just one song I could sing,
Of Jesus Christ—earth's great Majesty—
I'd sing at Christ's birth, my welcome to earth.
God's sweet song of Salvation's liberty!

I would rejoice about angels and shepherds.
I would sing of the wise men who came.
I would celebrate the star created for earth-birth,
Of Jehovah's great Son—Jesus named.

Shout loud hosannas in the highest heavens.
Jesus as Savior comes, God's best to re-claim.
A Bethlehem birth—a Jerusalem man—
God's only Son Savior—Lord Yeshua named.

Tell all the earth, God's story called Christmas.
To the earth shout God's song of great praise.
Lift God's anthem to men, the Son comes again.
His jubilation/salvation song heavenward raise:

Jesus—God's Son—comes at Christmas.
God's only Son—Jesus—rescues His earth.
Eternal Salvation—called Yeshua—is here.
Sing eternal song of Redemption's glad birth!

Eternal Word Conceived

Jesus Christ—eternally God—
By Shekinah of God Most High,
Came to a body prepared for Him,
To draw all men God nigh.

As Gabriel announced her "favored,"
Mary received God's Holy Word.
"Let all be done as you have said!"
…her womb God's Word secured.

Mary by faith God's Son conceived—
The One, Whom at God's right hand stood.
No promise e'er broken; as the prophets had spoken.
Eternal Word, in flesh was robed.

Majesty intact—powers limited—
LOVE came, the Man to serve all men.
All God…all Man! All Man…all God!
Incarnation/Substitution for sin.

The Firstborn of Mary

Jehovah the Son, our Savior He comes.
He is Son of God—the Firstborn of Mary.
To Bethlehem led, a manger His bed,
This humble Messiah our sins soon shall carry.

In Mary's womb, Jesus to Bethlehem was borne.
God's plan to rescue man, Mary obediently bear.
Into a Roman world in Bethlehem hurled,
Jesus—God's born-human Son—love shared.

God's first Christmas to Bethlehem came,
As the Hebrews their captors obeyed.
For centuries proclaimed our Savior, Christ came,
To Bethlehem Ephrata, just as Micah conveyed.

A Jewish Baby into a Roman world born,
Only our God could have brought it to pass.
Jesus is Lord Messiah to all the world.
That first Christmas our God showed such class!

For Easter to Bethlehem Come

Reflections at Easter on the Bethlehem birth—
Intervention of God in coming to earth.
Jesus the Messiah—born behind the inn—
Came as the Creator, His creation to live in.

Mary and Joseph with Jesus had come.
In Bethlehem Ephrata, God's plan was begun.
Rescue, redemption, completion, restored.
God's purpose for man was Jesus as Lord.

A Bethlehem birth for a Jerusalem cross.
Easter was planned as part of the cost.
Jesus came as a Babe. He grew up the God Man.
Resurrected from the dead new beginnings He planned.

Now all creation can be Jesus's blood redeemed.
The Glory of Easter is Christ's birthday presence esteemed.
Freedom from sin came by the death of God's Son.
By His incarnation at Bethlehem deliverance has come.

For Spirit Body and Mind

Christ the Lamb, Jehovah I AM,
Savior holy and just, Lord Supreme.
Give us Your grace and heartaches erase,
Make us to reign as Your holy redeemed.

At Christmas we honor the Spirit,
That caused Mary to boldly say,
"In Your grace I stand. I am Yours to command.
I honor You. I am Yours today!"

Mary, Joseph, and Jesus our Lord,
Were Bethlehem faithful for all mankind.
God's kingdom has come in power,
Receive strength for spirit, body, and mind!

From Mary's Womb

Gabriel first said, "Yeshua comes!" in Galilee…
The Holy Spirit overshadowed virgin Mary.
The Word was conceived, taking on flesh.
And nine months passing, drew Bethlehem breath.

From Mary's womb in Bethlehem,
A Savior came forth, named Yeshua the Lamb.
God kept His First Garden promise.
That night the Eternal Seed, was born the Man.

Yeshua has come as Father's Love-Gift.
Our hearts are love-prompted, great praises to lift.
To the Yahweh of Israel, Our Creator Supreme.
Coming to Bethlehem's manger…mankind He redeemed!

Full-Peace Christmas

Yeshua was sent by our God, for His man.
On a peaceful night, Full-Peace began.
That nothing be missing, Shalom has come.
Crown-Prince Shalom is God the Son.

Revealed-Jehovah, whom Jerusalem keeps,
In lowly stable, their Shalom Prince sleeps.
Jesus—Prince of Peace—as Messiah arrived.
The Lamb—love sent—Full-Peace provides.

Christ bore our sin, sickness and lack to hell.
Claim Full-Peace provision—live Full-Peace well.
For your total wholeness Prince Full-Peace died.
Have a Full-Peace Christmas in Jesus the Christ.

Full Redemption to Provide

Kneel at the manger, view there God-Babe,
Who came to earth your life to save.
At the foot of His /cross, watch Him die.
His empty tomb… "Resurrection!" cries.

The Christmas Babe…His life subsiding,
By His Cross death was Life providing.
He opened to all a crimson tide—
Full redemption to provide.

For you the Lord of Glory came,
A righteous robe to give and change your name.
Christian…Christ-won! This Babe has come,
To birth righteous God daughters and sons!

Give Glory to God in the Highest

Give glory to God in the highest…
Peace on earth…good will to men.
Jesus the Savior is born in the earth,
  The wayward to Father to win.

All worship Jehovah Yeshua,
Rejoice! He as Savior has come.
To give righteous robes, in wee swaddling clothes.
Now incarnate is Yahweh the Son.

Welcome the Lord of Creation to earth—
The Christ Child…the Savior of Men.
Sing, "Glory to God in the highest!"
All creation…all angels…all men.

Shout! "Glory to God in the highest!"
Give glory to God evermore.
Sing "Glory to God in the highest!"
Christ Jesus the Savior is born!

Give Him Due Praise

Give glory to God in the highest!
Give glory to God all the earth.
Welcome Him in, the Savior from sin.
Celebrate Messiah the Lamb's humble birth.

Give glory to God in the highest!
Rejoice! This Babe is our Lord-Evermore.
Give Him due praise. His love anthem raise!
Lord Yeshua ha Mashiach adore!

Shout, " Glory to God in the highest!"
Sing, "Glory to God evermore!"
Salvation has come. Full-liberty He has won.!
Jehovah-Our-Yeshua, forever adore!

God Our Peace Has Come

Heaven's high host hailed shepherds,
"Glorious news: God our peace has come.
Let all creation celebrate earth-birth,
Of Jehovah God the Son!"

Give Him honor...God-Babe in the manger.
Sing high-praise to this Great-Shepherd King.
Hosanna to God in the highest, lift high,
Lord-Incarnate...Full-Salvation now brings!

This Lord of Creation is Jesus the Christ.
Salvation to the masses He brings.
Exalted our Lord. In heaven adored,
His worship-filled praises we sing!

God's Christmas Delight

He's the Savior of men, this Child born this night.
The Almighty, Savior, Creator, and Guide.
To us He comes. He will set things right.
He is Messiah Redeemer, God's Pride.

Out back in Bethlehem's humble stall,
The King of Creation has come.
To usher in peace and a kingdom unleash,
Comes the Ruler of all—Jehovah the Son.

Mary and Joseph we honor your Child.
Faithful are you both to God's plan.
As Savior Jesus comes. God's will be done.
In this stall, birth Redemption as planned.

Shout from the rooftops in Ephrata,
A Savior to our world comes this night.
He is Jesus Lord Christ, our eternal life.
His man restoring, He's God's Christmas delight!

God's Christmas Gift

We have received a Gift from God.
He is much more precious than gold.
God's Gift will live eternally.
To all men, His Gift will be told!

This Gift is Truth in human flesh—
Our Savior Jesus Christ—
To cleanse from sin revealed to men,
That blessed holy night…

Where the God of Truth and Justice—
In love, sin debt to pay—
Became the Seed of Woman…born,
God's Gift on Christmas Day.

This Gift of gifts is King of kings—
The only Savior…Christ!
God's Christmas Gift; He lives to lift,
All men to righteous life!

God's Grand and Glorious Story

Heaven's Crown to Earth come down…
God's grand and glorious story.
Lord Jesus Christ to pay sin's price,
Now enters human history.

Christmas is Messiah Mass—
Earth's "freedom-now-comes" celebration.
Joy to the world the Lord has come,
To purchase full salvation.

Give glory to Jesus the Christ.
The Ruler of Heaven, the Author of Life.
Let Jesus be exalted as Savior Supreme.
There is none like our Savior. Jehovah redeems!

God's Infant Meek and Mild

Great joy to all in every land,
There is a Savior Christ the King.
Declare His name. His birth proclaim.
His sweet Salvation sings.

With angel hosts rejoice this hour,
Then with shepherds view this child.
He is King of Kings and Lord of lords,
God's Infant meek and mild.

Mary, Joseph, Jesus Christ,
God's threesome on love's mission.
With these three agree eternally.
Celebrate Jesus's birth at Christmas.

God's Master Plan

God's master plan to rescue man,
Sin's wage and causations to cease.
Meant Jesus must give Himself as the Lamb.
Full Salvation—spirit, mind .and body to release!

It was no surprise to Jesus Christ,
The condition of man that He found.
God's Infant Son King, Salvation would bring,
Redemption expressing His whole world round.

This Christmas celebrate full Redemption.
Total Salvation take as your own.
As you are giving your gifts, Jesus's name lift.
Seek God's face. Share the might of His throne.

Jesus coming to a stable at Christmas,
Means full power of our Lord we can know.
Let us live fully free eternally,
Knowing the God-kind of health—living whole here below!

God Son of Mary

He is Jesus our Savior Messiah,
Our Redeemer, the Restorer of earth,
We celebrate His birth—His coming to earth—
Establishing forever His glorious worth.

Tell of His coming to Bethlehem's stall.
Tell how He rescues all men.
Proudly proclaim His wonderful name.
Exalt Him. Rejoice, Jesus your Savior came.

The name of our Savior is Jesus.
For as the Savior of all He is here.
God Son of Mary by Joseph secured,
With shepherds we rejoice as we share.

For unto us a Savior is born this night,
In David's royal Messiah City.
We will praise His good birth,
And welcome to earth the God Son of Mary.

Have a Jesus Freedom Christmas

There is freedom in Jesus the Savior,
In Bethlehem born this day.
All the glory of God abides in this Son—
And every son—who will Jesus's freedom convey.

You really celebrate Christmas best,
When the Savior you know in His power.
Your Christmas can be mightily free—
Holy Spirit filled with Pentecost each hour.

Have a Jesus freedom Christmas,
That lasts the whole year through.
Give yourself to Jesus' might.
The mighty works of Jesus do.

Jesus came to Bethlehem's stable,
Announcing God's holy freedom true.
Jesus the Messiah makes every Christmas free.
Let Jesus accomplish His Father's will in you!

He Finally Has Arrived

Jesus in eternal ages past.
With Father created the worlds.
Then when sin had come, Jehovah the Son,
Was determined sin's mess to unfurl.

Jesus' birth in Bethlehem's stable,
Was preordained—God's purposed Salvation plan.
Jesus our Lord in heaven adored,
Was sent to the earth to rescue sinful man.

Yes, Jesus—God's holy ancient Son—
New to this planet, for sin was now come.
We exalt Him this day to His prominence.
Happy birthday! Jehovah redeeming Son!

Merry Christmas! God be praised!
To this earth Messiah has come. Salvation is done!
Forgiveness, restoration, and healing of diseases—
Victory over sin is fully won.

He Makes Us Reconciled

As promised, the Savior,
To Bethlehem came.
And in Mary's mild voice,
Earth first heard his name.

He is Jesus to Christians,
LORD Yeshua to Jews.
Of David's lineage, He has come,
The Serpent's head to bruise.

Since He first spoke creation,
The earth, Christ Jesus loved.
Returning as LOVE-the-Servant,
He has our sins removed.

We now bow low to worship,
The resurrected Christmas Child.
We here embrace God's Christmas grace,
To be Jesus's blood reconciled!

Holy Ghost *Christ* Mass

We celebrate for a month the heaven-sent reason,
There is on earth presents giving season.
It takes thirty days of praise for Christ's birth celebration,
And eternity to reign in Jesus's full liberation.

Christmas begins Messiah's hell-crushing mission.
By Blood of this Man, Christ the Lamb's commission,
Is issued to those in The Christ anointing-might sent.
Father needed it done, so God the Son to Bethlehem's
stable went.

That is the total reason why Christmas is
The *Anointed's* Mass—
A complete-liberation, full-salvation,
Incarnation Celebration.
Christmas is best when Pentecost blessed, and the
Anointed One is embraced.
Born by His blood, caressed by His good, let His holy
Ghost *Christ* Mass take place.

Hosanna Liberation/Salvation

Hosannas lift high, God is with us to save!
Joy to the world, our full freedom is come.
As prophets foretold, no good God withholds.
Our God loves us. He sent us His Son.

Now all can really shout to God, "Hosanna!"
A praise to God, derived from, "Save we pray!"
Christ Jesus has come. God's Plan for full freedom,
At Christmas, Resurrection Day to convey...

Christmas—Celebration Mass of Christ,
For liberation/salvation Jesus came.
Easter...Christ died for sin then...resurrected to life.
At empty tomb..., Bethlehem's Resurrected full freedom
proclaimed.

Full-freedom for mankind is God's Christmas-born Gift.
To liberate God's man from sin-bondage Christ came.
The Bethlehem Babe your full ransom has paid.
Your total liberation/salvation Jesus obtained.

Humanity and Deity Together

An Eternal Being our Savior,
As Lord Immanuel came to earth.
At Christmas time in Gospel rhyme,
Proclaim Messiah's humble birth.

Humanity and Deity were together,
In the flesh of Christ the Word.
In that manger bed gently laid,
Was Jehovah Christ the Lord.

Incarnation of royalty,
Earth's future Sovereign sweetly slept.
As Father God choosing Bethlehem sod,
Four-thousand year Savior-promise kept.

Worship Jesus your Savior King.
To His manger-cradle praises bring.
With humble shepherds give Jesus laud—
This Eternal Being—Son of God!

Humble Birth
Majestic Messiah

"Glory to God in the highest,
And on earth goodwill toward men."
As the angels proclaimed, the shepherds—not doubting—
Went with haste to Bethlehem.

Mary embraced the joy of their greeting—
Holding deep in her heart her great awe—
For she also believed and greatly received,
Their confirming her Child, Son of God.

At his announcement Gabriel had promised,
She would carry the Son of the Highest.
Mary was pleased as JHVH Son slept.
Humble birth...majestic Messiah!

Humble Birth Regal Savior

To that little town in Ephrata province,
Mary and Joseph were taxation bound.
Arriving in Bethlehem there was no room.
In a humble stable this couple laid down.

It was not a grand palace for a Savior,
With no regal pillow for His head.
Our precious Savior would be stable born,
Having a simple, but warm, manger bed.

It was not our God Who had no room,
For a Savior to be regally born.
It was just the taxes with census,
And our Mary tired and slightly forlorn.

Joseph and Mary loved Jesus that night.
These proud parents their God Child adored.
God sent shepherds to Mary to say,
"It's a humble birth. He is a regal Savior!"

In Bethlehem Christ Adore

To the little town of Bethlehem,
Our Messiah came that day.
On a donkey borne, no inn-room for our Lord.
Mary carrying our Savior prayed,

"Give a humble bed, and a place of rest,
To the mother of Your Son speak peace.
Let Jesus be born before the morn.
Let Your Kingdom Lord God increase."

Mary the mother of our Lord had carried,
The prince of Judah to His birthplace.
She rejoiced in her God on the Bethlehem Road.
She thanked God for resting grace.

Born to you this night in the City of David,
A Savior who is Christ the Lord.
What a wonderful day. Bethlehem the place.
Merry Christmas to all. Christ adore!

–

In Bethlehem's Stable

In Bethlehem's stable—no inn-rooms remained—
The Messiah was born,
Where Prophet Micah proclaimed.
God's Son most exalted, the Savior of men,
Was born in a barn, behind the inn.

To Mary's discomfort, the stable was dank.
So drafty and noisy and mightily stank.
But Gabriel's grand message—nine months to the day—
Yet glowed in her heart, to melt her dismay:

"His Name shall be JESUS, the Highest own Son,
On David's throne to reign...the One!
O'er the house of Jacob, His kingdom unending,
By act of God's Spirit, within you beginning."

So Mary, God's chosen, gave birth to His grace,
For she was His servant, and this was the place,
Where the darkness of sin, would first view the Light,
Through gentle submission, to heaven that night.

The King of Creation, Almighty enthroned,
As Father desired, was seeking His own.
Counting men worthy—all creatures above—
The Sovereign of earth was serving in love.
Yes! Down from His radiant throne of might,
Heaven's Crown, bowed low that night.
That He might ransom sinful men,
And raise them up, to reign with Him!

In the Glory of Angels Announced

The angel of the Lord came to them.
The glory of the Lord shone round about.
"Fear not", said he, "Great tidings of joy,
 To each tongue and tribe I shout:

"Unto you this day a Savior comes,
 His name is Christ the Lord.
This shall be to you a special sign,
A Babe in swaddling clothes you'll find,
 Lying holy in a manger."

Suddenly a multitude appeared—
 A host of heavenly creatures.
Praising God, this host decreed:
"Glory to God, on earth great peace.
Good will from heaven to men be known.
God's great mercy will never cease."

Jehovah Yeshua to Bethlehem Come

Christmas the holy birth of Lord God the Son—
Jehovah Yeshua has to Bethlehem come.
Born in a manger, the Savior of men,
His purpose for coming, a lost world to win.

It is definite decision of our Father God,
To redeem from all nations His people by blood.
Incarnation—The Lord our God made man,
In Bethlehem's stable the start of God's plan.

Salvation is new standing by the total cost,
Jesus paid to redeem us and save from loss.
Salvation is rescue—the saving from lack,
Restoring to virtue. Dominion giving back.

Every sin gone—entirely removed.
Filled with God's Spirit. Full authority renewed.
Jesus the Savior has to Bethlehem come.
Christmas the birth of Jehovah the Son.

Jesus Came

Christmas is a special time,
To celebrate Jesus in song and rhyme.
We are rejoicing because our Savior has come.
In Bethlehem born—Lord Jesus, God's Son.

Yes, born in a stable—in a manger bed laid—
Jesus came to earth. He provision made…
That all our sins be placed on Him.
Jesus came that night, our freedom to win.

All of God's goodness resides in the Lamb.
In his name and His blood every man stands,
Totally forgiven, healed and set free.
Take liberty in Jesus for eternity.

All of your days of sinning gone,
You are totally God's. You in Jesus belong.
Ransomed, redeemed, healed and made whole,
There is freedom in God, when Christmas Savior controls.

Jesus Come to Us

Mary's little Baby—Jesus the Christ—
Our Creator-Redeemer, grand Author of Life.
Born in a stable—Your soft bed the hay—
You have come here to save us this day!

We adore You our innocent Savior sweet.
Born in a barn, You came down to redeem.
Thankful to Your mother, our hearts are blessed.
We worship You Jesus, our Savior Supreme.

Messiah magnificent, prophesied come,
We prepare now our hearts as Your home.
With angels and shepherds, You here we welcome.
Love us our God. By Your blood sins atone.

Jesus Lord Redeemer, Messiah esteemed,
By Your Father sent, we welcome You King.
Lord Jesus our Healer, mighty Author of Life,
We praise You. We yield to You our lives.

Worship-filled praises to Jesus belong.
Merry Christmas to all, our love-season song!

Jesus the Eternal Be Worshipped

Worship Lord Yeshua
Praise His holy name.
Declare to all, before Him fall,
And never be the same.

He came from Father's presence,
To the little barn behind the inn.
He spent the night there with His mom,
As Joseph welcomed the shepherds in.

Glory to God in the highest!
Praises eternal in Bethlehem!
He's Jesus, God's Son—to this stable come—
Exalt Him Lord forever this day.

Jesus the Eternal be worshipped this night.
Rejoice all the earth in Salvation delight.
Eternal His glory, resurrected the Lamb.
Praise Him forever His glory proclaim.

Jesus Lord Messiah to Bethlehem Come

Jesus, Lord, Messiah to Bethlehem come,
We worship You Savior, Lord Redeemer the Son.
Sent from Your Father, You purchased by blood,
You rescued us ever. You eternally loved.

To Your manger bed, shepherds were led.
We honor You, Lord, alive from the dead.
You came here to seek, to find, to save.
We thank You, Redeemer, for the blood that You gave.

Lay soft in Your manger, waiting that day,
When Galilee behind, You kneel to pray:
"Father, take not this cup that I drink away.
I am redeeming them forever. Your will I obey."

Jesus our Lord sleeping, rest on... faithful be.
You have come here to rescue. Our redemption we see.
Lord, God, Messiah, Lord Lamb to be slain,
We honor You. We worship Your rescue name.

Jesus Our Messiah Lord

We worship Jesus, God the Son!
To save us all this dear One comes.
Laid in a manger is our Messiah Lord.
Jesus, coming to this stall, we highly adore.

We worship Jesus born this night.
For He is the One Whom Father delights.
This Mary—His mother sitting by—
Is that hurting one who will watch Him die.

Her soul will weep in years to come,
But she bows this night to hold God's Son.
Her heart of love has her God obeyed.
She carried the Christ. She our Lord conveyed.

We kneel with Mary beside this Child,
Who will bear our sins and reconcile…
Us back to God to be restored.
We worship Jesus our Messiah Lord!

Jesus Our Redeeming Lord

Jesus Who came to Bethlehem's stable,
In Jerusalem would soon be heeded.
It was a wonderful day, God to obey.
Anna and Simeon decreed our Salvation completed.

They worshipped this Child as the Son of God.
He was Salvation in human flesh arrayed.
Simeon declared Jesus the Savior of might.
He called Jesus Salvation! Simeon heaven obeyed.

We too can worship this Jesus the Christ.
He is the God-Man of Israel declared in God's Word.
A Bethlehem birth for a Jerusalem King.
Circumcised as Yeshua, is Jesus our Redeeming Lord!

Jesus the Son of God's Love

He is Jesus, Jehovah's dear Child.
He is Jesus our Lord from above.
We worship this Savior who comes,
Messiah Jesus, Jehovah's dear Son.

He came here to guide us to heaven and hope,
To place in our hearts Father's love,
He is Jesus Messiah, anointed to serve,
And redeem us to God by His blood.

He came here loved, He's Jehovah our Lord.
Shepherds have heard their Messiah is here.
They now come to adore Jesus, their Lord,
Assembled to worship, to praise, to revere.

Shepherds on hillside, by angels called in,
They honor this Jesus the Savior Lamb.
He is Jesus our Messiah anointed to serve.
He redeems us to God by His blood.

Jesus We Honor You

Jesus our Messiah, to Bethlehem come,
We offer to You our glad praises.
Such a beautiful Babe. You have come to save.
We honor You in worship-filled phrases.

Jesus born in Bethlehem's stable,
We honor You this special night.
We give You glory Yeshua Lord.
We rejoice in Your saving might.

Jesus, Bethlehem Ephrata You honor,
With Your presence meek and mild.
With shepherds we sing praise to our King.
We honor Jesus who heals His reconciled!

Joy to the World

Glory to all nations, your Messiah here comes.
To Bethlehem, shepherds by angels are drawn.
Praise His great Name. This child now fame.
In Judea, Galilee, and Jerusalem His glory dawns.

This One is Lord Messiah, Shepherd King.
Eternally through the ages worship Christ.
On this holy night, in God's Son delight.
He is our Creator, our Savior, our Light.

Joy to the world, a Savior is born!
Joy to the world, Christ Jesus is life.
We praise His great name, and gladly proclaim,
Let all the world worship Jesus the Christ.
Born Son of God and infant Savior this night.

Joseph Are You Listening?

Joseph are you listening?
Joseph can you hear?
There are those who hate this Child.
So hear My voice sincere.

Arise and flee to Egypt.
Take there this holy Child.
Jesus, Son of Mary protect.
Dwell in Egypt by the Nile.

Take you gifts of frankincense,
Fine gold and holy myrrh.
There is peace for you till Herod's through.
Dwell in Egypt safe secure.

Out of Egypt bring My Son to Me.
To My Israel now make haste.
I am most sincere, My voice now hear.
In Nazareth He will be safe.

Know Jesus Know Christmas

Celebrate Jesus coming to Earth.
At Christmas rejoice in your Lord.
Tell your kids and grand little ones,
"At Christmas Christ Jesus adore."

Say boldly, "Know Jesus—know Christmas."
Give Christ honor. Have a grand Christmas season.
Reflect on your Savior's Bethlehem birth.
Choose redemption—God's great Christmas reason.

For a celebration as grand as Easter,
With its resurrection from death to life.
Celebrate! Rejoice, it is Christmas—
The Birthday of Jesus Lord Christ!

Jesus came to Bethlehem's stable,
To make me a son, fully free.
I celebrate His birth and His living.
Jesus is Christmas, Easter, and Pentecost to me!

Let the Festival Start

Highest of Heaven, Lord of all lands,
In Your grace and mercy, delivered we stand.
Precious sweet Savior, our Salvation supreme,
We rescued, rejoicing, are fully redeemed.

In Bethlehem born, the Savior of men,
We kneel low before You, welcoming in.
Let the festival start. Let Your glory begin.
Redeemer, Savior, all creation You win.

Your great mercy and power forever we sing.
Yeshua You are Lord, almighty great King.
You come here to serve, resurrect, and set free.
You are King of Creation—Redeemer of me.

I will shout salvation. Freedom comes in the Son.
In Bethlehem's stall is where it began.
Almighty Redeemer, Savior Supreme,
We bow to Your power as Your birth we esteem!

Live Christmas Each Day

I enjoy a Jesus freedom Christmas,
In the might of my Father divine.
All power of Christ Jesus—Bethlehem born—
By Jesus's shed blood is eternally mine.

From Bethlehem, Ephrata to Galilee come,
His might exceeded that of the Sanhedrin boys.
Though born in a stable this Jesus is able,
All might of His Father to fully employ.

Journey with me to Bethlehem's stall.
There view the holy Son of God.
As you linger there, your alliance declare,
With Jesus' redeeming/healing Blood.

Make this a Jesus freedom Christmas,
In your Jehovah-Jesus the Christ.
Live Christmas each day as you Father obey.
Yield to Jesus your abundant new life!

Lowly Comes the Word

To the town of Bethlehem,
Lowly comes the Word.
And we with shepherds bow to praise,
This Child—Jehovah LORD.

To Bethlehem for Calvary came,
This humble Prince of Peace.
No other One has true love lived,
And can from sins release.

We see beyond these stable walls,
Into the heart of God.
We praise Jehovah-Father God,
For the Christ Child's saving blood.

Thank You, LORD, for Bethlehem,
And Your Seed who came to die.
His Blood our only cure for sin…
We yield to Him our lives.

Magnificent, Majestic, Almighty I Am

Messiah Majestic in manger bed,
Rest in peace. Decree God's best.
As Savior You come to Bethlehem,
That all the world may be blessed.

Creator, Redeemer, Savior, Lord,
We honor this night You are born.
We praise Your Name and Your kingdom proclaim.
Grant this world Your peace in her storm.

Messiah, Savior, Redeemer be praised.
Be exalted. Your kingdom may it never cease.
We celebrate Your blood, God's Gift of Love.
We crown You our Prince of Peace.

Shepherd eternal, Savior Supreme,
By Your precious blood all nations redeem.
Honor and Glory to Yeshua the Lamb—
The magnificent, majestic, Almighty I AM.

Make Haste to Bethlehem

Out on the Judean hillsides so vast,
It was a very calm and gentle night.
There was a wonderful peace, the moon glowed bright.
It truly was a beautiful evening, a glorious delight.

The sky was glowing God's brilliant display.
The moon in its splendor, shown as the day.
All was quiet. Some shepherds rested, while others could not.
Yes, this night would be special—not soon forgot.

For out in the distance—several green knolls beyond—
There seems to be a rehearsal to burst bright the dawn.
The horizon, seems to hum—like a murmur of sorts—
What are they saying in their choral report?

Look, it seems they are moving, they will soon be near.
We must listen so carefully, their message to hear.
Rejoice in high heaven, shout hosannas aloud.
There is the glory of heaven in this choral crowd.

O holy night, the stars are shining bright.
It's My time you see. This Child is Me.
Bring now My longing heart great delight.
It is My desire you hear My choir that you see.

Shepherds make haste to Bethlehem.
There see this Child, born a King to reign.
With this choir rejoice. Now heed My voice.
I—this Child—am God. Christ Jesus is My name!

Mary...Joseph...the Lamb

Was there a warm fire in the stable?
There was a love flame in her heart.
Mary, you carried True Love to the world.
We thank you, loving mom, for your part.

First Christmas morning, dear Joseph,
The God-Baby you loved, sleeping lay.
It was a sin-crushing partnership.
Thank you, Joseph, for the love you obeyed.

Christmas was LOVE's humble entrance in time.
From eternity, was first Christmas planned.
What love was conveyed. What a difference they made,
These three agreed: Mary…Joseph…the Lamb!

Mary's Baby Loved

A manger holds a newborn Babe.
His mommy laid Him there.
She cuddled Him and wrapped Him in,
Sheep wool the shepherds shared.

She loved her little Baby Christ,
To her womb from heaven sent.
He was a special holy Child,
To Mary till manhood lent.

She would give this precious Baby love.
Love deserved by God the Son.
She would teach Him right and wrong,
Then release Him. God's will be done.

Mary, love your Jesus Christ.
Hold Him close and sing your love.
As you hold Him, give Him ever to God.
That he might for all men, sins remove.

Mary's True Love

Thank you, Mary, obedient virgin of God.
You carried True Love in your womb.
You loved Love at birth. You loved Love in life.
You loved at Love's cross, and you loved in the upper room.

Mary, thanks for hearing the angel by love.
Thank you for submitting in your spirit.
Your heart held Love. Your womb bore Love.
Love you conveyed. He is True Love—we hear it.

True Love came to earth, by Mary's true love.
May we all to God's True Love be true.
God's True Love from above, Mary carried by love.
Obedient virgin of God, at Christmas, LOVE came via you.

Mediating Messiah

Mediating Messiah, Yeshua great Friend,
By Your precious Blood, eternity we spend,
With Abba our Father, Creator, and Guide.
By the power of Your Spirit with You we reside.

You are the Yahweh of Judah, Creator, and Lord.
Matchless Redeemer Whom salvation affords.
Father endless ages—eternity through—
We will bow to Jesus, giving honor to You.

Jesus came to that stable—a Bethlehem barn—
To rescue from Satan and preserve us from harm.
Jesus, Lord Yeshua our Savior esteemed,
We are forever forgiven...restored...blood-Redeemed.

With Mary and Joseph we worship our God.
Eternal Salvation the great gift of His blood.
With shepherds, then wise men, we honor our King.
Of gold, frankincense, and myrrh You are worthy, we sing.

Messiah Eternal Has Come as God-Man

As angels ring the stable that cradles Earth-King,
Heaven's choir cries forth, David's Promised, earth is in.
"To Bethlehem come, now your Messiah to see.
As Jehovah decreed, He is born in the inn!"

The Messiah eternal has come as Godman,
The sin-bound of creation by ransom to win.
Let His angels adore Him—do likewise all flesh—
The Chief Shepherd comes lowly…the Lamb for lost men.

This infant Christ-King deliverance brings,
To humble shepherds, innkeepers, and priests.
Forever in song, His grace greatly praise.
His great reign in bowed hearts will never cease.

Hosanna! Our Savior—Lord Yeshua—has come.
Let all, of wisdom, now worship God's Son.
Give glory all created to Elohim High.
Alpha and Omega, your Redeemer has come!

Messiah Give Great Awe

Jesus the Son of Mary is,
Yeshua the Son of God.
Precious Holy Spirit born,
That God might shed His blood.

That is the Christmas story.
God incarnated as the Word.
When the matchless Lord of Glory,
Took on flesh to be earth's Lord.

Come with me to Bethlehem.
Worship your Savior in the straw.
Look into His eyes of love.
Your Messiah give great awe.

Kneel before the King of kings,
For mankind come to earth.
Forsake your sin and enter in,
To His kingdom by new birth.

Messiah We Embrace You

Jehovah Lord Yeshua to Bethlehem come,
We honor Your presence; we worship God's Son.
Such an honor to know You—our lives Blood Redeemed.
We worship You Yeshua our Jehovah Supreme.

Recounting Your journey to Bethlehem's inn,
We crown You with worship great Messiah our Friend.
In our God resting, we sing praises to Jerusalem's Savior.
We thank You for coming—born new—us to favor.

Mary and Joseph with holy angels we sing,
Jesus is Savior and Healer, our Shepherd Supreme.
Messiah we embrace You, our lives at Your feet.
How blessed to know You, and be made complete.

This our grand message forever shall be,
"In Jesus all are worthy—made whole—blood freed."
No other is worthy. To the Lamb we lift praise.
Worship and honor, to You Lord Yeshua, we raise!

Millennium Christmas

Glory to God in the Highest!
His Kingdom will not cease!
He is God the Son—Immanuel come—
Christ Jesus…Prince of Peace!

A millennium of Christmas,
The Living Word shall bring…
From David's City, Heaven's Crown,
Will reign the King of kings.

One thousand years of Christmas joy—
God's Peace on Earth shall reign—
As Jesus Christ the Savior rules,
The world for which He came.

"My-Anointing in You!" Is Christmas Truth

Glory to God in the Highest!
Wholeness/peace for men on earth!
Yeshua ha Mashiach, Lord Savior, I come!
My wholeness-anointing, celebrate in mirth!

Bring them to Me! Restore them in Me!
They mourn for My salvation.
It's all been done—their victory is won.
I bought their liberation.

Tell My story! Tell My plan…
Resurrection-win declaring!
They only know when My sons go—
My full-salvation sharing.

Bring them My Life, begun this night,
Two thousand years preceding.
"My-anointing in you!" is Christmas truth.
The Christ of the Mass, all the earth is needing!

No Other

Jehovah we now worship Your Son come to die.
We exalt Him as Maker Messiah from on high.
We humbly behold Him, we love on His neck.
He as truest Lord Redeemer—Son of Mary—we respect.

No greater Redeemer from our Father could come.
No other is worthy to be Lord Messiah, God the Son.
To Bethlehem Ephrata our Savior descended,
He spoke of Father's great love. He never offended.

He proved to us all our Father was love.
He bowed on the earth to transport us above.
None higher is anywhere mentioned as Lord.
This humble Messiah salvation affords.

To the Yahweh of Israel this anthem we raise.
No other is greater. Lord Jehovah be praised.
Lord Jesus restore us. Make us all, Your-blood new.
Thank You Father our Redeemer is our Yeshua true!

No Other Is Worthy

The joy of the Lord Jesus Christ proclaim.
There is resurrection might in the power of His Name.
No other is worthy like Jesus the Lamb.
The Lord our Savior-Jehovah I am.

Come let us worship our Savior, Jesus the Lord.
Let us bow at the altar of Heaven's Highest Adored.
None is worthy like Jesus, Creator, and King.
Of our praise He is worthy. His greatness we sing.

All hail our Lord, Yeshua the Christ.
We will surrender in worship, to the Author of Life.
Heaven is waiting but now on the earth,
We will honor the One Who has purchased New Birth.

All hail the King! All hail Christ the Lord!
Forgiver, Restorer, Enricher of Life!
There is none like our Savior-Creator-Lord!
Give all the honor forever to the Lord Jesus Christ!

No Room...Good Mother

Christmas in Bethlehem—the very first one—
Where will our Savior be birthed?
There are nowhere any rooms in an inn.
There is no place worthy it seems in the earth.

Then a mother-to-be finds protection in a stall.
It is a stable—so noisy and damp.
The inn-keep's servant is helpful and kind.
This place seems too humble, but God's helper I am.

Yes, here in the back, I'm removed from the crowds.
Though it is damp the hay will be warm.
Jehovah with me His Son soon shall see,
And Joseph will keep Him from harm.

I am Mary His mother...faithful—His friend.
The Savior of men is born to me this night.
No room in the inn, but Salvation shall win!
In the good mother of Jesus, our God will delight.

On Our Way to Bethlehem

We are on our way to Bethlehem,
Baby Jesus to see with Mary.
We rejoice as we go for this we know,
This Child our sins will carry.

Bethlehem—peaceful David's city—
In you Messiah is born.
We are pleased to see His majesty,
On this, His after-birthday morn.

Throughout eternal ages,
The world will plainly see,
Bethlehem of Ephrata,
God's kingdom springs from thee.

Your taxation/census filled God's purpose.
God's prophecies pass as written.
God's Kingdom has come in His dear Son.
Freedom from sin God's world is gettin.'

Our Christmas Majesty

Heaven rejoiced. The shepherds made haste,
To Bethlehem to see.
A Child in birth-clothes humbly placed—
Our Christmas Majesty!

We rejoice in God's Redemption Plan—
Christ restores from Adam's Fall.
We choose the Lamb of Bethlehem.
We on His goodness call.

Majestic Christ Child, Prince of Peace,
Death choosing to make us free,
We crown You now, our King of Peace—
Our Christmas Majesty!

Our Great Redeemer Is Given

Born in Bethlehem the Son of Man,
He is Jesus the Savior come to us this night.
We worship Him this holy Lamb.
He is majestic. He rules in might.

The King of Creation to Bethlehem comes,
Bringing salvation and glorious peace.
Our Jehovah reigns our Redemption One.
His great kingdom will never cease.

Down through the centuries revelation reigned,
Proclaiming Yeshua ha Mashiach soon comes.
Every promise given is fulfilled in Jesus.
He to Bethlehem comes as Jehovah the Son.

Jesus is Messiah—Lord Immanuel—to us.
Shout salvation from rooftops of Bethlehem.
As our Savior He comes, our Messiah we trust.
To us our great Redeemer-forever is given!

Our-Hope-Eternal Shines

From Bethlehem's cradle,
The Woman's Seed, Our-Hope-Eternal shines.
Bringing peace, with God's full wholeness,
To all…born twice…renewed in mind.

We celebrate LOVE's humble birth.
We lift praise to our LORD from heaven.
By grace born again, we call all men,
To this Savior for all flesh given.

Our Lives Now Offering

Twas the night of the first Christmas—
The Bethlehem's stable, first one.
As the angels gave voice the shepherds rejoiced,
At the birth of Yahweh the Son.

Two years later came the wise men—
Astrologers, magi, kings.
We come this day True Wisdom's way.
Our lives now offering.

This Baby praised at Christmas,
We choose to love each day.
We yield our lives His love to live…
His anointing-gifts to convey.

Our Savior He Comes

He is Jesus Christ. He will conquer grave.
He is our healing One. He comes to save.
He is born of Mary in this damp inn,
He is the Christ, who comes to conquer sin.

See Jesus asleep on manger hay.
Our Savior He comes. He our God obeys.
We worship Jesus born this night.
He is the One who makes things right.

This Jesus lad born innocent,
Shall save each soul that will repent.
We worship Christ. We crown Him Lord.
This precious Babe by shepherds adored.

We rise to sing, "Salvation comes!"
This Child that sleeps is God the Son.
He comes for you. He will give His life.
Embrace your Savior—Jesus Christ!

Our Song of Salvation Singing

Our song of Salvation singing we come.
With holy angels glad tidings we bring.
For a Savior is born to us this night.
Christ Jesus, His holy name we sing.

He comes from heaven's portals,
To give us God's very best.
His purpose in coming to Bethlehem,
Is that all the world may be blessed.

Prophet's prophesied Him for centuries.
Jesus finally has arrived.
We praise You Lord Jehovah.
Your holy Son is precious in our eyes.

Mary Your faithful servant we highly adore.
Joseph beside Jesus stands so tall.
He is Messiah magnificently formed.
Happy Father, we give You thanks for it all.

Our Spirits to Redeem

We can all trust YHWH.
We may all bow down,
At Bethlehem's cradle,
God's Gift to crown.

Lord Christ our Creator,
Though Almighty Supreme,
Has come to Bethlehem,
Our spirits to redeem.

Jesus Christ our Messiah,
Savior, and Healer fore'er,
Has kneeled in Bethlehem,
His love to share.

Bow low before Him,
Worship Him there.
At Christmas, His birthday,
Your loyalty declare.

Pascal Lamb Child

The fall of First Man, in First Garden,
Came after Father's First Option first mention.
Great the sin that would come, requiring First Son,
To shed sinless blood for Redemption.

Love promised was confirmed in First Garden.
The Seed of the Woman would be LOVE's plan—
That with God-Man body and blood,
Her Seed would become Paschal Lamb!

Long centuries came. In darkness man dwelled,
Till God's time for Paschal-Blood finally came.
By Abba sent, to womb...to cross...and a tomb,
True love has come....Lord Yeshua the Savior His Name!

His love altar was a Cross. His tomb empty lays.
With God's angels give glory-filled praises to Jesus.
To set all men right, First Son was born of Mary that night.
He the paschal Lamb Child, man reconciled.
By Paschal Lamb blood, He redeems us.

Pentecost Christmas

Pentecost Christmas, is true Christmas for man,
As the Spirit of Mercy and Might, fully planned.
Deliverance from Hell by the blood of the Lamb.
No sickness or lack allowed in the land!

The Christ Child ministered, Shalom-Peace to the earth.
Rejoice in the Anointed One's Bethlehem birth.
Celebrate God's goodness. This Christmas proclaim,
Christ's anointing so mighty, it melts sickness chains.

Christmas Pentecost bounty means more than enough.
Like young Mary of Galilee, The Anointing One trust!

Pentecost Christmas Power

In Christ's birth month hell's hordes confront,
With the truth of Pentecost Christmas power,
That enables the once lukewarm to celebrate,
In the Anointing One of Christ, at Christ's birth hour.

Have a Messiah mirth celebration of Christ's birth.
Since Resurrection Morning receive heaven's might on earth.
Be God's Pentecost power anointing endued.
Receive by the Holy Spirit heaven's might in you.

For the greatest Christmas celebration alive,
You must in your spirit receive the living Christ.
Then celebrate His ushering in as your Redeemer Friend,
By His Pentecost power released in your life!

Please Welcome Him In

Merry Christmas! Merry Christmas!
Celebrate the birth of Jesus our Lord.
Declare in the Earth Messiahs grand worth.
Rejoice in Jesus, shout praise, in Yeshua rest assured.

It is a time of great rejoicing in Bethlehem.
The casting off rebellion as sin melts away.
In this stable this day God's love is displayed,
As freedom and health come our way.

Good news to all people everywhere,
He is a Messiah Lord of freedom born this day.
He is Jesus the Christ the Author of life.
He has come our sin to erase. To Bethlehem make haste!

Yeshua-Eternal, the Savior, has come,
To the barn behind Bethlehem's inn.
He is our emissary of grace, all sin to erase,
He comes for you; please welcome Him in.

Praise Him The Savior Eternal

Praise Him the Savior Eternal,
Praise Him the Lamb that redeems.
Worship His name, His goodness proclaim.
Praise the Lord God Eternal Supreme.

Praise ye the Lamb all you peoples,
Declare Jesus is Savior and Lord.
The One Who has saved us and ransomed our lives.
Praise the Lamb. Praise the Lord. Praise His Word.

Give all the glory to Jesus.
Worship and praise Him His holiness.
Our Savior who came. Our Healer proclaim.
He is majestic, our Friend. Praise His name.

Blessed be the great name of Jesus.
Blessed be our Savior Redeemer.
Our Healer. Our Blesser. Our King.
Worship Yeshua, as Savior.
Worship Him. True praises bring.

Preparation, Adoration, Exaltation, and Room

The story has gone to every land.
To Bethlehem Jesus the Messiah comes.
He is here to save and make hearts to brave,
Declaring to all, Redemption in Yahweh the Son.

Mary and Joseph from Galilee for tax,
Now decreeing we are the lineage of David.
We have come this night for it is right,
And we are to the Romans behavin'

Shepherds on hillside hear the Lord,
As God's angels declare Christ's birth.
"Unto you in the city of David is born,
The Savior who will cleanse the earth."

None other higher than this dear Son,
Delivered tonight from Mary's womb.
Welcome Him in. Give yourself to Him.
Give preparation, adoration, exaltation, and room.

Prince Total-Freedom

Christ's humble birth began,
Earth's True-Liberation Plan.
He came to begin Abba's,
Eternally-Loved-Ones-Kingdom!

Love-the-Son's earth mission,
Is earth-sphere liberation.
In Christ-Celebration declare,
The birth of Prince Total-Freedom.

Proclaim Yeshua's Birth

Shout O Earth! Burst forth in praise!
A joy-filled shout in Judah raise.
He Who comes shall save from sin,
Usher Prince Yeshua in!

Make room for Peace—Yahweh Shalom.
Adore Earth's King, O Jerusalem.
Angel hosts have come His birth to fame,
This night proclaiming Yeshua's name.

Forever all sinners should jubilant be,
For God has come all men to free.
Leaving heaven's opulent, eternal wealth,
God comes to His earth to offer Himself!

He is Abraham's Seed, born Judah's Lion.
Jehovah the Son has come to Zion.
Lift thanks-filled voices all over the earth.
Eternally proclaim The Messiah's birth!

The Redeemer I Am

Messiah He comes to Bethlehem's manger,
Brothers to birth whom once were strangers.
All men He seeks in meekness this night.
This Baby who sleeps will set things right.

Rejoice throughout ages eternal,
Your Messiah is here born King.
He will ascend to the throne of Heaven Supreme,
For He reigns Lord Savior, the King of all kings.

Happy we linger with shepherds to say,
The Almighty Creator dwells with us this day.
Let all of creation worship the Lamb,
Jesus the Messiah, the Redeemer I AM!

Redeemer Lord Savior

Who is this Jesus asleep on the hay?
He is our Redeemer, Lord, Savior we say.
He is Jesus of heaven now dwelling among,
The chosen of Father, who rest in the Son.

Jesus, Yeshua ha Mashiach, the Lamb,
Has come here to find us. We with Him now stand.
He will save, heal, and restore us,
Deliver, and set free, our Redeemer Christ Jesus.

God our Savior, our Redeemer, highly esteemed,
We praise You, we sing: "Your blood has redeemed."
Destined for heaven with Jesus we stand.
We will worship You ever Christ Jesus the Lamb.

In Bethlehem's stable, the start of our race.
By Jesus we are God's—blood-purchased of grace.
It started in Bethlehem with Mary and Jesus.
No other Name under heaven, ever can free us!

Redemption Pledge to Fulfill

Hallelujah! Praise Jesus the Lamb!
Worship Jesus our Savior who came.
Proclaim His great worth in all the earth.
Jehovah Yeshua His Salvation name.

Tell to the children a Savior is born.
This Savior to redeem you has come.
He is Jehovah's great joy, Mary's little boy—
Jehovah Yeshua the rescuing One!

Give praise to Yeshua throughout the earth.
Worship and praise Yeshua the Lamb.
This eternal One, as Jehovah here comes,
To reign Lord forever, the Redeemer I AM.

Bow at the manger in Bethlehem.
Kneel at Christ's cross on Golgotha hill.
Where this Delivering One, for your freedom has come,
God's Redemption pledge to you to fulfill.

Reflections...On the Bethlehem Birth

Reflections at Easter on the Bethlehem birth—
Intervention of God in coming to Earth.
Jesus the Messiah—born behind the inn—
Came as Creator, His creation to live in.

Mary and Joseph with Jesus had come.
In Bethlehem Ephrata God's plan was begun.
Rescue, redemption, completion-restored,
God's purpose for man was Jesus as Lord.

A Bethlehem birth for a Jerusalem cross.
Easter was planned as part of the cost.
Jesus came as a Babe. He grew up the God Man.
Resurrected from the dead, new beginnings Jesus planned.

Now all of creation is Jesus's blood redeemed.
The glory of Easter is Christ's birthday presence supreme.
Freedom from sin came by the death of God's Son.
By the incarnation at Bethlehem deliverance has come.

Restoration by a Child

How precious this Son of Jehovah was born here.
As Messiah we worship Him—God's very own Child.
By Mary He was carried beneath her heart,
Son of Man He comes, God to His man to reconcile.

Incarnation—God as Godman He lives.
Sweet God-Babe Mary gently held in Bethlehem.
Within her heart from this day forward.
Affectionately night and day she cherished Him.

God's perfect Plan in a garden was begun.
Manifested in flesh, Second Adam He comes.
God had instructed. Angels had obeyed,
Loudly speaking, "The Gift of God is to mankind conveyed."

Worship the Christ One meek and mild.
Honor your Lord Jehovah the Child.
Mary and Joseph God you obeyed.
God's reconciliation-beginning is made.

Soon to die on Calvary's cross,
At Christmas He comes to heal our loss.
"Be reconciled to God. Peace on earth!" through angels
is spoken.
God has restored forever what Satan had broken.

Rise up Early to Bethlehem Go

Rise up early to Bethlehem go,
The Messiah will be there, at His birthplace most low.
There all of the glory forever is His,
For as our Messiah, Jesus ever shall live.

He is Almighty Redeemer, Jehovah divine.
In Yeshua ha Mashiach wholeness we find.
The peace of the ages, will be our portion extreme.
For He is the Righteous, who fully redeems.

In Bethlehem Ephrata the prophet declares,
Our Lord Messiah will make His birthplace there.
Humble and merciful, majestic and grand,
Behold Him. Adore Him, Yeshua the Lamb.

Come all of God's children from the ends of the earth.
He is Lord God Messiah in Bethlehem birthed.
With Mary His mother and Joseph His dad,
What a glorious Redeemer, is this Savior lad!

Salvation at Christmas

Jesus the Messiah, King of the Jews,
To Bethlehem came an infant child.
Mary and Joseph brought Him there.
His world from sin He came to reconcile.

Centuries before it was prophesied,
That Bethlehem would be His birthplace.
No room in the inn. He came to bear sins,
Hate, heartaches and despair to erase.

Shepherds on hillside were called to observe,
This Savior Child in swaddling clothes.
How they noised abroad that the Son of God,
Was born in the place six hundred years earlier foretold.

Now every year we commemorate the birth,
Of the Bethlehem Babe come to reign.
Celebrating far and wide, rejoicing we cry,
"He is Jesus our salvation!" At Christmas Christ came.

Salvation Comes

He is Jesus Christ. He will conquer grave.
He is our Healing One. He comes to save.
He born of Mary behind the inn,
Is Christ who comes to forgive our sin.

See Jesus sleeping on manger hay,
Sent as Savior He comes our way.
We worship Jesus born this night,
For He is the Christ. He makes things right.

We rise! We sing, "Salvation comes!"
This Child that sleeps is God the Son.
He comes for us. He will give His life.
We embrace our Savior, Jesus Christ.

Savior Come from Above

Jesus, Yeshua, Savior, dear Lord,
What a tremendous treasure Your love.
We thank You forever for coming to earth,
To fit us for mansions above.

Our sins Blood-removed…made heaven approved,
In renewed hearts Your love-heart You placed.
O glorious Love come from above,
You we worship, from hearts…pure by grace.

Born new by Your blood…wrapped in pure love,
By Your Spirit, now Your earth-touring home.
How wondrous to be joint-heirs and free,
Till blood-faithful we kneel at Your throne.

In blood-freedom we lift, praise for love-gifts.
What glorious enfolding Your Spirit affords.
In praise blessing our journey to Your heaven-pure peace,
We worship You, Yeshua our Lord!

Savior Forever Supreme

Redeemer, Savior, Healer, Salvation revealer—
Jesus the Messiah, Jesus our Lord.
There is power in his name. His glory proclaim.
Abide in His love. Honor His holy Word.

He is deliverance, wholeness, completeness,
Of provision, nurture, and health.
Who will declare Him, with others to share Him.
There is none like our Master of opulent wealth.

Rejoice and be glad in His presence.
Declare Him the Lord of all lords.
There is none like our King. He ever Redeems.
Sing Jesus is Savior forever Supreme.

Who will excitedly worship with praise,
The Lamb that was slain for healing and sin?
Open your life to the Lord Jesus Christ.
Invite the King of Creation within.

The Savior for Men

How greatly rejoices this grand angel host.
Announcing tonight in bright form:
"To all and for all, comes this your great King."
For the Messiah to Bethlehem Mary has borne.

Christmas celebrates earth birth of our God—
Who for our salvation visits His earth.
Here to shed for all flesh, His redemption-pure blood.
Confirming forever, man's blood-purchased worth.

Christ Jesus, Mary's Baby-beautiful born—
Who in Bethlehem slept softly that night—
How joyous our song, for to You belongs:
All creation! All glory, All might!

A Savior Is Born
in Bethlehem

A Savior is born to the world this night.
Bethlehem the scene of wisdom's might.
Celebrate this Jesus, Bethlehem born.
Son of God—our Savior—Him adore.

We shout from Bethlehem's stable, truth.
Humble shepherds receive Him in a stall.
Lord Jesus sleeping silently expresses,
God's glorious song of freedom to all!

It happened long ago. Let the whole world know,
Salvation is calling to everyone:
Have yourself a merry Christmas,
Here in Bethlehem's stall begun.

Come kneel to the Savior in Bethlehem.
Rise up with Him for Galilee freedom.
Rejoice in Jerusalem, there occurs a resurrection.
Through Bethlehem's Jesus, be a part of God's kingdom.

The Savior of Men

There's a celebration in the stable,
Behind Bethlehem's inn.
For the Sovereign there cradled,
Is the Savior of men.

Sweet Mary how special,
This Charge in your keep.
This matchless Messiah,
Salvation shall preach.

We come to adore Him,
To bow at His bed.
For He is our Savior,
To die in our stead.

From heaven to Calvary,
To hell in our place.
This message Christ carries,
"God's Christmas shouts GRACE!"

The Savior Our Redeemer Has Come

The truth be told in Mary He rode,
This Infant Son from heaven come.
Jesus the Christ, God's wonderful One…
Son of Mary, Lord Jehovah the Son.

We come to Bethlehem's cradle to worship.
We journey to welcome our Jerusalem king.
There we will know God's Salvation has come.
His strong light to the nations to beam.

In Jerusalem, Jesus we worship as Lord.
Thirty years hence to Calvary our traveling takes us.
At the garden tomb Resurrection shines forth,
Sons of God, in His glory formed, He makes us.

To Bethlehem, Egypt, Nazareth, the world,
The Savior our Redeemer has come.
We rejoice with angels, we celebrate His birth—
Christmas, Easter, Pentecost—Jesus' fame!

A Savior Who Is Man

How can a Savior who is Man be our God?
How can we ever be this loved on earth's sod?
Just, You the Savior, great Mediator Supreme,
Could come as the Godman, our lives to redeem.

In a Bethlehem stable, a manger His bed,
Jesus came here to serve us. He died in our stead.
Here we observed Him, this Healer so kind.
Our Savior, our Redeemer, our Blesser Divine.

Father in heaven, this Jesus we love.
We thank You for sending Your Son from above.
From your heart, dear Father, this Savior proceeds.
Thank You for Jesus, His words, and great deeds.

There is none like this Savior in Bethlehem sleeping.
No greater Redeemer our souls could be keeping.
Jesus, Lord, Creator Redeemer Supreme,
We thank You for heaven and blood that redeems.

Shalom to All

With shepherds—like later wise men—
We embrace what the angels proclaimed:
"There is shalom complete in Mashiach…
Great joy in Yeshua's name!"

"Shalom to all!" this Mashiach Mass,
JHVH Yeshua has come.
Completeness-wholeness anointing flows,
As we celebrate God the Son.

Shelter Enough and Secure

Mary and Joseph to Bethlehem came,
Weary of the dust of the road.
Bethlehem was so busy—no room in the inn.
With-child, weary, dusty, discouraged, Mary groaned.

"So sorry, it is the taxation. I'll ask a maid.
There is a stable out back. It will be free...except,
There is a fee for your donkey's keep,
And the sheets, blankets, and pillows, I regret."

"You have come to our town when we're so full.
My stable is the best I can do.
Be warm, be careful, be blessed my friends.
You are so pregnant. When are you due?"

Bethlehem Ephrata, Bethlehem most loved,
In you tonight a great birth occurs.
Mary, I am with you. I love you my sweet.
It will be shelter enough and secure.

Song of Christmas Joy

I will sing a song of Christmas joy,
To Jesus Christ my King.
I will sing a song of Christmas joy…
His praises I daily bring.

I will worship Christ who came to die,
And set sin-captives free.
I will honor Yeshua of Bethlehem,
For His wondrous love for me.

I will worship daily at the feet,
Of Jesus Christ my Lord.
I will live my life in happiness,
Sheltered daily in His Word.

From Bethlehem let hosannas rise,
To the cross of Calvary.
With shepherds and angels praise this Babe,
That shares His glorious liberty!

Sweet Mother of Jesus

Joseph his beautiful bride hugged.
So grateful, Mary whispered her love.
Joseph the afterbirth quickly removed.
Jesus graced the manger...heaven's Approved.

Thank you Mary! What a wonderful Child.
Joseph was so tired. He had not slept.
Then the shepherds arrived...chaos controlled.
Joseph cared for Mary. An angel promise kept.

Sing hosannas! Rejoice Messiah Mom.
Nine months behind, you are blessed to find,
Gabriel was correct. Son of God Jesus sleeps.
Mary, Mother of Jesus, our Savior has come as designed.

Goodnight sweet Mother of Jesus.
All nations will call you blessed.
You rode that donkey all those miles.
You delivered the Savior Child. Take your rightful rest.

Their Infant Lord

Simeon and Anna received the Word.
The Messiah—God's Anointed—had come!
That Baby born King of Israel,
To God's holy temple carried was Jehovah God the Son.

This was the Crown Prince of Israel,
In the flesh arrived, God's glory He revealed.
Circumcised as Jesus on His eighth day,
For His purification, to the temple He was carried.

This Salvation and Redemption Babe,
Truly was Jehovah's sinless Son.
Anna and Simeon both agreed,
This was God's Anointed holy One.

They took great pleasure in their mission begun decree.
Jesus the newborn Son of Mary,
Was both Creator and Messiah.
Their infant Lord Yeshua, descended from on high.

They Remember the Christ-Child Born

Christmas comes each year in Bethlehem.
They remember the Christ Child born.
They recollect Mary, Joseph, and Jesus,
A threesome on holy mission Jesus' birth-morn.

Author of eternal Salvation born,
In Bethlehem's barn that night,
Was a lowly child in manger mild,
Revealed in glory, splendor, and might.

Wrapped in swaddling clothes this One,
Brought pride to Joseph's bold exuberant smile.
He and Mary had done things well.
How they loved Him—this sweet gentle Child.

A few days hence in Jerusalem,
The splendor of it all was fully known.
As Simeon and Anna by the Spirit confirmed,
This Child was God's Anointed, bringing Redemption
to His own.

Thirty Holy Days
to Celebrate

It takes thirty holy days—not the famed twelve.
To celebrate correctly this royal birth.
When the majestic Crown of heaven came down,
To fully liberate His man and His earth.

Be filled with the Holy Spirit of Christmas.
The holy Anointed came to earth this night,
To resurrect from sin's-death, earth's residents,
That they could live fully-free, in Christ Mass might!

The Spirit and His Anointed celebrate.
December 25th...the Julian date.
Receive the Messiah—the Christmas God-Child.
Crown Christ your Savior. To God be reconciled!

Receive *Christ* Mass might.
Receive the Christ this poem tells.
Let Messiah Jesus give you freedom from hell.
(Christmas born; Easter raised; He Pentecost sent;
then home went).
Crown Christ Lord at His cross. Sinless rise to His throne.

This Child in Betlehem Born

Who is this Child in Bethlehem born,
Laying in manger on clean hay?
Could this be the One from heaven come,
To bring in God's Full-Restoration Day?

Is this the Savior of all mankind?
Is He destined to reign as a King?
Is this the Messiah of David's royal line?
Is this Jesus of whom holy angels sing?

Glory to God in the highest, their heavenly song.
All splendor, all beauty endless ages belong,
To this Child born the eternal of God,
Offering Sacrifice of His saving blood.

Who will declare Him? Who will lift praise,
To the Yahweh of Judah, Ancient of Days?
Yeshua ha Mashiach, Bethlehem's holy Son,
As Savior and Lord to be adored He comes!

This Child Who Is Savior and Lord

Since the dawn of creation, no greater elation,
Have the angels of God e'er conveyed.
For Father delights in proclaiming this night,
High Prince and Lord-Savior…this Babe.

No angels before have so greatly adored,
A more righteous King, rightly crowned.
For this Baby born King, Redemption shall bring.
Let our Lamb-Savior's praise much abound!

From the East to the West, Salvation caress.
Let Crown-Prince of Redemption be adored.
For from throne room of God to Judean sod,
Came this Child who is Savior and Lord!

This Day the Christ Was Born

How are things in heaven above,
This peaceful Christmas morn?
How are the angels rejoicing,
This day The Christ was born?

Are angels by the Spirit dispatched,
Great grace to speak in unison above?
Are they saying far and wide, "Christ came!
Fulfilling Father's plan of hope and love"?

Below the earth is bustling with celebration strong.
Everywhere people choirs offer up joy-filled Christmas song.
Let all of the earth rejoice with heaven above,
Declaring to all God's eternal love.

Jesus' birthday is here, let us spread good cheer.
Because sin and sickness are removed, rejoice!
Celebrate, celebrate, Christmas celebrate!
Let all the earth embrace God's choice.

For by His Son God's kingdom comes—
Let present-day saints and angels lift glad voices.

This Day a Savior Is Born

We sing our song of salvation,
Like those holy angels proclaimed.
To us this day a Savior is born.
Christ Jesus is this Savior's grand name.

He comes down from heaven's portals,
To give us God's excellent best.
Jesus' purpose in coming to Bethlehem,
Is that all His world may be blessed.

This Jesus is born for Calvary.
To die for sin and sickness he is carried.
Mary, God's chosen, obedient in birth,
Our Redeemer here brings to rescue His earth.

Jesus our Reconciler back to God,
Your eternal purpose…eternal blood.
You forgive all sin, making whole and free.
Healed spirit, soul and body eternally.

You are Jesus our Savior, Creator and Friend.
We worship you Jehovah, eternity we'll spend,
With the Infant of Bethlehem,
This majestic Redeemer I AM.

This Great Savior Sleeping

Who is this great Savior,
In a Bethlehem stable?
Our Alpha and Omega—
Our Salvation in a cradle!

Sing His Song of Salvation,
The angel host loud proclaimed.
Our great Savior sleeps softly.
To save us Jesus came.

Salvation has come to all men,
The angel choir voiced as song.
We come to Bethlehem to worship.
All praise to our Redeemer belongs.

He is Lord and Messiah,
Come to save us, our song.
This Jesus is so worthy of worship.
All the praises of heaven to Jesus belong!

This Jesus I Love

Full blood-provision Jesus has made.
In Jesus I am forever blood-saved.
I am fully-free in the blood of the Lamb.
A Blood-redeemed new creation in Jesus I am!

There is none like our Savior, Jesus the Lamb.
God's chosen, eternally is Jesus I am.
I am set fully-free in Jesus the Christ,
Heaven's Great Ruler—the Master of Life!

Nothing I desire while living on earth,
Is more important than this Jesus I love.
Though I gained the whole world, I would surrender it all,
To be redeemed—bought back— by His blood!

I am born to the purpose of serving Lord Christ.
He died in my place—for me sacrificed.
Let us bow together to Jesus—the infinite Lord Son.
We shall reign in His love and the victory He won!

To Bethlehem for Me

To Bethlehem He came for me,
My Savior long ago.
Since He came I'll live forever.
I will His awesome presence know.

Jesus is my Savior's name.
To Bethlehem for me He came,
That I might know eternal love,
And the glory of His matchless name.

Tremendous is God's care for you.
Eternal is His holy love.
Give Him your sin, receive His grace,
Which sin, sickness and lack removes.

Come with me to Bethlehem,
Bow before His manger bright.
Let Jesus, Joseph and Mary be thanked,
As the Spirit of Christmas your spirit makes right.

To Forgive Sin and Make Us Whole

One more Christmas psalm for our Savior.
Another Christmas verse for our Lord.
We will worship Him—this Savior of men—
Born to a manger in Bethlehem.

Mary and Joseph found no room in the inn,
As they carried our Lord to Bethlehem.
Yet born this night in David's city,
Is the Son of God, the first born of Mary.

We worship this newborn as Christ,
Offering praise and thanks to Yahweh.
For this Savior of men, born in Bethlehem's inn,
We shout praise to heaven this day.

We give all the glory to our Father God.
Life's Author is the Restorer to life.
We the Ancient of Days in Bethlehem praise.
He is Jesus Lord triumphant—the Christ!

We Honor the Lamb

We thank You loving Father, for sharing Your Son.
Thank You for Mary and Joseph here come.
With angel entourage and shepherds, we adore,
Your Son in Bethlehem, Yeshua the Lord.

Great innocent Baby our sins soon to carry,
We lovingly caress You like Joseph and Mary.
None other is worthy great Jehovah I AM.
Our lives in Your Book, we honor the Lamb!

To Judea and Galilee, to Egypt and return,
We honor this Jesus. We embrace and yearn,
We ever draw near Him with worship-filled words.
We crown Him Redeemer, Mashiach the Lord.

Jesus to Nazareth, then to Calvary's crest.
Our lives at Your feet, we are Jerusalem blessed.
Honor to You Jesus, the Eternal we sing.
Made worthy are we. We are fully redeemed!

Who Is This One?

Seven days hence He will not be known,
As the newborn Son of Mary.
But the Savior come, God's holy One,
Jesus our sins to a cross to carry.

Who is this One asleep on hay,
Whom for shepherds to worship has come?
This little One by Joseph here led,
On the donkey is Yeshua, Mary's Messiah Son.

Who is this One from heaven come,
King of shepherds this holy night?
Worship this King. His praises sing!
In Yeshua ha Mashiach delight!

Sing glory to God in the highest.
Let peace on earth abide in you and me.
Worship this heaven-sent lad. Rejoice, be not sad.
He is Jesus—God's Son—our victory!

Wise Men

When the wise men got to Jesus,
There was no manger, and no hay.
It had been a troublesome journey,
With setbacks along the way.

When the wise men looked on Jesus,
He was sitting in a fine high chair.
By Joseph designed, it was buffed and shined,
It complemented the fine lad there.

Two years had passed with no fanfare.
This Jesus Messiah was not widely known.
No one exclaimed His Savior name.
No one had offered this Boy-King a throne.

Though your talk with Herod informed,
You certainly were not wise men that day.
But how could you know that coward would throw,
A fit—every two-year-old life to take away.

How can we know what the wise men knew,
As they left gold, frankincense, and myrrh.
All that we know is that God favor showed,
While the rest of history is blurred.

Wise men decreed this Baby will free.
He is Savior to bring us full liberty.
He is Lord, Yeshua, Creator and Lamb—
Our Jehovah, the Shepherd I AM!

Wisemen to Jerusalem

His name shall be called Jesus.
He will save our souls from sin.
He is our Lord Immanuel.
By His Blood we know no sin.

Following a star that led to Jerusalem,
Magoi told of Jesus' birth in Bethlehem.
Then borne from the East great gifts they gave,
As the two-year-old acknowledged them.

We want to be scripturally sound.
Wise men heard no angel resound.
At Bethlehem's stable—let's get it right—
Wise men still traversed from afar that night.

Their gifts of gold, frankincense, and myrrh,
Were presented at the time of Herod's rage.
Soon Joseph escaped with Jesus to Egypt,
Using the wealth by wise men staged.

The World's Savior in Bethlehem

Jesus the Savior to Bethlehem came,
As the righteous, holy, newborn of Mary.
Here He was Jehovah Lord God,
The Blessed One, God's servant carried.

Down from heaven and worshipped as due,
Came Jesus the Savior that holy night.
To Bethlehem's stable the Messiah was brought.
The Holy Spirit was pleased—delighted.

Who can gaze at this Savior Lad,
And not be pleased God to earth has come.
The angels decreed God's Savior we'd see,
Let us worship Jehovah the Son.

Yes, the Spirit of the Lord had descended,
And shown His light on the womb of Mary.
At the Word of the Lord Mary was pleased.
She the world's Savior to Bethlehem ferried.

Worship at the Stable First

Sing glory to our Father God.
Worship Christ Jesus the Son.
Thank God for His precious gift,
New life in Christ begun.

Worship at the stable first.
Then worship at Christ's cross.
Praises give that Jesus lives,
To rescue every sinner lost.

Our song of total Redemption lift,
To our Savior Jesus Christ.
Praise Jesus' s name. His love proclaim.
He has saved and healed our lives.

It all began at Christmas,
In Bethlehem long ago.
With Mary and Joseph rejoice,
The Christmas Babe you know.

Yeshua Lord King

Outback is the stable where Jesus arrived.
With Mary and Joseph, Jesus in Bethlehem abides.
Jesus this Messiah to Ephrata comes,
To save us from Satan and make us God's sons.

The shepherds heard angels and forthwith they came,
To see the Messiah their Yeshua named.
The angels in unison spoke, "Your God find,
In a cradle in Bethlehem with cattle and kine."

Mary and Joseph as Father demanded,
Had come obedient to Micah's command.
In Bethlehem Ephrata let the whole world see,
There is One who is born all nations to free.

Worship in Bethlehem God's holy Child.
He has come to His world all to reconcile,
Back to the Father who created these beings.
Let Jesus be worshipped as Yeshua Lord King.

Yeshua the Prince of Peace

Enmity between the serpent's seed,
And the offspring of the woman.
Destruction reigned since Eden everywhere.
But a Messiah came to Bethlehem.

Unto us is born in David's City,
A Savior which is Christ the Lord.
The Kingdom of God on His shoulders rests,
This wonderful Counselor, Living Word.

Jesus is Mighty God. He is Everlasting Father.
He is Yeshua the Prince of Peace.
Born David's Son all nations to bless—
His kingdom everlasting will never cease.

Yhwh-Yeshua the Lord

The King of Creation, touching earth this night,
Cleaves history forever in glorious might.
In your Lord Who is Savior, forever delight.
For incarnate He comes to give you His rights…

The right of salvation and the right to new birth,
The right to glean His harvest—the redeemed of the earth.
Christ Jesus from heaven all creation adore,
For Jesus this Baby, is YHWH-Yeshua the LORD!

Your Christmas Savior

Crown earth's Christmas Deliverer, your Savior Lord Christ.
For His purpose in coming was to rescue by His
shed blood,
Those in sin-bondage living dead, from the great fire
lake ahead.
Christmas-born for substitution at Calvary came
God's Lamb of love.

This glory-filled season called Christmas is a great
time to reflect,
Why would Jehovah send from heaven His Most
Loved for me,
To live as a Man without sin and then die carrying mine—
Bearing my death-penalty, to give me His Zoe eternally?

Make your conclusion your inclusion in
Christmas Redemption.
Christ Jesus of Christmas—God's Resurrected—
now living, give honor.
Embrace your Messiah. At Christmas, God's new
species become.
Do not a sinner remain. Awake…new life gain in
your Christmas Savior.

Testimony

In a Gaston, Oregon house,
Our Savior's plea was made.
In answer to that call,
A simple prayer was prayed.

Daddy was the preacher,
Of a humble sermonette.
Responding to God's call,
This child Dad's Savior met.

Bowing at a chair,
An altar there we made,
As son and dad together,
To their Father prayed.

Our Father heard my prayer—
A contrite sinner's plea.
As I asked in Jesus' Name,
God took my sin from me.

And that's the special reason,
I share these poems with you;
That you might choose to make,
My Lord your Savior, too.

--Robert E. Scrivner

www.ingramcontent.com/pod-product-compliance
Lightning Source LLC
Chambersburg PA
CBHW072009090426
42740CB00011B/2146